THE INDIAN STORYBOOK

Rani Singh

ILLUSTRATED BY BRYAN ORION

HEINEMANN : LONDON

For my son
Jairaj Bir Singh
from Rani

For Tansy and Dylan
from Bryan

William Heinemann Ltd
Michelin House
81 Fulham Road, London SW3 6RB

LONDON MELBOURNE AUCKLAND

First hardback edition 1984
First paperback edition 1988

ISBN 434 96332 1

Printed in Hong Kong
by Mandarin Offset

Contents

Introduction

INDIA has a culture and a religious history going back over thousands of years, linked to a tradition of storytelling which is equally old. The stories of gods and goddesses, kings and queens, poor men and saints have all been passed down through the ages, changing and evolving to meet the needs of each generation. The timeless and universal qualities of each tale keep it alive and vibrant even today and each of the stories in this book can be found in one form or another all over India.

Storytelling was a very important part of my childhood. My sister, brothers and I would listen to the wonderful myths and legends told to us by my mother and grandmother, and I grew up with a love of the spoken word. It is now my aim to make available to everyone this treasury of tales to which I was first introduced as a child. I give many performances of Indian stories to children with my husband, Jugnu, and like storytellers throughout the world, we adapt them and give them our own colour and dramatic expression.

The eight stories in *The Indian Storybook* are not intended to be definitive versions. Some of them have never been written down for children before, but they are all favourites of mine – and of my young audiences.

I would like to thank my parents, Parsan and Harbans Singh, for all they have done and continue to do for me, and for giving me a strong awareness of my own cultural heritage. Without their help, and the great support of my husband, Jugnu, this book would not have been possible. I am also grateful to Mr B. C. Bloomfield, Director of the India Office Library, Mr P. A. Nazareth, Secretary to the Indian Council for Cultural Relations and Dr I. P. Singh, Indian Ambassador to Spain, for their invaluable assistance.

Rani Singh, March 1984

Many different gods and goddesses are worshipped in India. Here are the ones who appear in *The Indian Storybook*:

Vishnu is one of the most important Hindu gods. He is the preserver of the universe and teaches goodness and mercy. Fine-looking and strong, Vishnu is married to the goddess, Lakshmi, and Hindus believe he has come back to earth nine times in different forms to save mankind from evil and suffering. Two of these forms were as Krishna and Rama.

Krishna, called 'the teacher', is one of the most popular Indian gods. He is fun-loving and good, killing demons and protecting cows and herdsmen. Many stories about Krishna are told in the epic legend, the *Mahabharata*.

Rama is regarded as the perfect model for all men – brave, good, kind and noble. As king of Ayodhya, he was a fine ruler and his period of kingship was known as the Golden Age. Rama's story is told in the great epic poem, the *Ramayana*.

Sita represents goodness, virtue and loyalty. She is the wife of Rama and is another form of Lakshmi, wife of Vishnu. She also appears in the *Ramayana*, and is the goddess of agriculture.

Hanuman is the son of the god of the wind and a holy nymph. He was devoted to Rama and was the leader of his large monkey army. He is renowned for his intelligence and holiness and is a very popular god.

1
The Magic Lake

IN THE KINGDOM of Rajasthan there once lived a rajah who had three daughters. The youngest, whose name was Purnima, was sweet-natured and obedient, but her sisters were jealous and scheming.

One day the oldest sister said, "I am going to marry the richest man in the whole of India."

The second sister said, "I am going to marry the most handsome man in the whole of India."

They both turned to Purnima and waited to hear what she would say.

"I will marry whoever my father chooses for me," said Purnima.

"She's just saying that to please you, father," the wicked sisters scoffed. "She doesn't really mean it."

"I do," said Purnima. "I will obey my father."

So the sisters teased and tormented Purnima until their father intervened. "I believe Purnima would marry whoever I chose for her, even if it were a ragged beggar," he said.

"Then prove it!" cried the wicked sisters.

And so determined was the foolish rajah to prove how obedient his beloved daughter was that he said, "Purnima, I command you to marry the first beggar you meet outside the city gates and to go away and live with him as your husband."

So Princess Purnima was forced to leave the palace. As she went out of the city gates, there in front of her on the ground in a huge wicker basket, sat a small, ugly beggar. This was the man her father had commanded her to marry!

With a sigh, the princess looked at the miserable creature, whose head was misshapen and whose limbs were deformed.

"Hello," she said to the beggar.

"Hello," he squeaked back. He had a thin, strange voice and stared up at the princess with large, unblinking eyes. "I can't walk. Will you carry me?"

Princess Purnima was gracious and kind, and felt sorry for this poor creature. She picked up the basket and placed it on her head. The load was heavy but he was her husband, and now she had

no home she had no choice but to take him with her. Purnima walked out of the huge gates and away from the city. Carrying her husband in the basket on her head, the princess trudged from town to town. She worked and some days earned enough money to feed her husband and herself. She grew thinner and thinner. Her clothes became tattered and torn. But Purnima cared tenderly for her husband and even grew to love him.

One hot day, they came to a lake.

"It's so hot, princess," squeaked the creature in the basket. "Why don't you leave me here by the edge of this lake in the shade of the mango trees while you go off and find some food for us?"

"Very well," said Purnima. "I won't be long."

Carefully she lowered the basket from her head, placed it under a tree by the water's edge, and set off to the nearby town.

Her husband sat in his basket and watched the birds and dragonflies round the lake. He saw an ugly black crow fly down to the water to drink and to bathe. It disappeared below the surface. The beggar waited for it to fly up again. Seconds passed, and the beggar's mouth dropped open in amazement, for the crow was nowhere to be seen. Instead, a white swan rose effortlessly out of the water. The ugly crow had changed into a beautiful swan!

The beggar could hardly believe his eyes. "This must be a magic lake!" he said to himself. "How could a crow change into a swan?" And if the lake had the power to change creatures, perhaps it could change him. Perhaps, if he too bathed in the clear water, he would become healthy and normal as he had once been. If only he could reach the water! He looked round desperately for help. There was not a soul to be seen. Even the swan had flown away. What could he do? He had to get to the lake!

He placed his arms on the sides of the basket and began rocking from side to side. Soon the basket was swaying violently. One more heave, the basket tumbled over and the beggar fell out onto the ground.

Slowly, painfully, he pushed himself the right way up. Using his elbows for support, he scrambled down to the edge of the lake. The water looked cool and inviting, but deep enough to drown in. The beggar crawled in. He immersed himself completely in the magic water, leaving only the tip of the little finger of his left hand untouched.

Then a wonderful thing happened. The beggar felt, and saw, his limbs become straightened. He felt life flowing into his legs. He was healthy, handsome and strong again, as he had once been. Joyfully, he strode out of the water and stood by the basket.

Just then the princess returned from the town, a bag of food in her hand. She looked at the basket. It was lying upturned where she had left it. There was no sign of the poor crippled beggar whom she had left behind. Instead, a handsome young man was standing there, smiling, one hand on his hip, the other outstretched towards her.

The princess's eyes filled with tears. She thought this man must have killed her husband. "Where is he?" she cried. "What have you done with him?"

"I *am* your husband. He is not dead," said the young man. "You see, my sweet one, this lake where you left me to cool off is a magic lake. It has the power to change living creatures. So I decided to try my luck and managed to get myself down into the water. And look what happened!"

"How can you expect me to believe that?" said the princess. "You must have killed my husband and now you're lying to me."

"I knew you'd find my story hard to believe," replied the prince (for so he was). "So I deliberately left one part of my body out of the water when I bathed, to prove that my words were not false. Look."

He held up his left hand and showed her the tip of his little finger. It was dark and misshapen, and the princess recognised it as belonging to the man she had married.

The prince walked to the edge of the lake and dipped his finger in the water. The princess watched in silence. As the prince held up his hand again, Purnima saw that the tip of his little finger was now smooth and strong, just like the rest of his hand and not crooked and ugly as it was before.

"Now do you believe me, Purnima?" said the prince.

He went on to explain that, many years earlier, an evil witch had placed a curse on him, and turned him from a prince into a poor deformed man, forced to beg for a living. But with the true love of a noble princess, and by bathing in the magic lake, the curse had been lifted and the prince restored to his normal shape.

"But through all these hard months, after being banished from your father's palace," said the prince, "and without knowing who I really was, Purnima, you have loved me and cared for me like a truly devoted wife. Come back with me now to my palace where you shall be crowned queen and I will surround you with

all the love, comfort, happiness and wealth that you deserve. This is my promise to you, my Princess Purnima."

The prince held out his arms and Purnima, overwhelmed with happiness, ran into them.

The prince did indeed keep his promise to his wife, and, as you can imagine, they lived happily ever after.

And to this day, the lake is said to have special healing properties, and is a place of pilgrimage for those who believe in miracles and fairy stories.

ॐ नमो नारायणाय

2

How Naradh was Taught a Lesson

VISHNU, THE ALL-POWERFUL, all-seeing god of the Hindus, could do many things. He could change into a man or a woman, or a tiger or an elephant, or even a stone. He was able to split himself into many different shapes all at the same time and appear to humans all over the earth in different disguises, whenever or wherever he was needed. Today, Vishnu is famous for his beauty and strength and is worshipped by all Hindus, who believe he will come to save the world from evil forces.

One of his worshippers was Naradh, who thought a great deal of himself and made a great show of praying to Vishnu every day by the riverside. He would go around telling everyone about his good deeds and lengthy prayers. He even began to compare himself with the mighty Vishnu. When that happened, Vishnu decided that it was time Naradh was taught a lesson.

Naradh was in love with the daughter of the king of a neighbouring kingdom and wanted to marry her, but her father had already arranged a swayamvara to find a husband for her. All the young noblemen and warriors in the land were invited to attend, and the one the princess considered the most handsome would win her hand in marriage. In those days, when one of the kings of

India thought it was time for his daughter to marry, this was what was done. He would hold a great feast, with music and sports, and the princess would choose a husband from among the guests.

Naradh was proud of his looks and thought himself quite dashing, but he realised there was only one sure way of beating the others in the competition and that was to look like a god. Vishnu, the creator of all things, was handsomer than any mortal man. If Naradh could only look like him then he would be certain to win the hand of the princess.

So Naradh prayed to the great god and told him of his love for the princess and of the competition to be held in the palace the next day.

"Lord Vishnu, you are the most handsome being in all the universe," said Naradh. "See how your body gleams in the sunlight, how strong and manly you look! Oh, Lord Vishnu, no one has worshipped you more faithfully than I have. Will you help me? If you could lend me your body just for one day, I know I would win the competition."

Vishnu listened to Naradh's pleading and replied, "I will grant you your wish." Naradh looked down at his arms and legs. They were strong and handsome, just like Vishnu's own. He was very happy, sure that he could win the competition at the swayamvara now!

The next day Naradh took his place at the palace of the princess in the long line of young men who had come from all over the kingdom to take part in the marriage contest. There were short ones, tall ones, fat ones, thin ones, handsome ones, ugly ones. Some had long noses, some had enormous ears. Some were richly dressed and others came in rags. Each hoped that the beautiful princess would choose him for a husband.

Naradh stood in line, confident that he was the best-looking suitor there. A fanfare of trumpets sounded, and the old king and his daughter the princess appeared. The king announced that the princess herself would decide who was the most handsome young man present, and he would become her husband.

The princess slowly walked along the line of young men. She looked at each, then moved on. She passed Naradh without even a second glance. When she had seen all the young men, she shook her head sadly and said that no one present was really worthy to marry her.

Naradh was furious. He said to the man standing next to him, "Why hasn't she chosen me? There's no one handsomer than I am."

The man looked at him scornfully. "You fool, you don't stand a chance," he said. "Haven't you looked at yourself lately?"

Naradh could not imagine what was wrong. He rushed into the palace garden and stared at his reflection in a pool of water. He saw the shining arms, legs and body of Vishnu. But as his eyes travelled upwards, he saw not the serene and beautiful face of a god, but the ugly head of a monkey.

Naradh staggered back, and felt with his hands the great mouth, the flat nose, the hairy ears and bulbous cheeks. As he slowly turned round in shame and fury, realising that a trick had been played on him, who should appear but Vishnu himself. He looked so magnificent that of course the princess fell in love with him at once, and chose him to be her husband.

Naradh was in a terrible rage. "How could you make such a fool of me in front of everyone?" he shouted. "What have I done to deserve it?"

"You were proud and bigheaded," Vishnu replied. "You told everyone you were worshipping me, but all you thought of was yourself. Your prayers were selfish and greedy, and I had to teach you a lesson."

Naradh would not see reason. He was angrier than ever.

"Well, Lord Vishnu, you think you are so high and mighty just because you are a god and can make me look silly," he stormed. "But I've some power of my own. I shall put a curse on you. You will come down to earth as an ordinary man, and fall in love with a beautiful woman. She will be taken away from you, just as you took the princess away from me, and it will be a man with the head and face of a monkey that will finally bring her back to you. This will be your punishment for the misery you have caused me."

And so it came to pass, as told in the story of Hanuman and Rama. Thus, though Naradh could not marry his princess and was humbled and humiliated by Lord Vishnu, he did get his own back on the great god in the end.

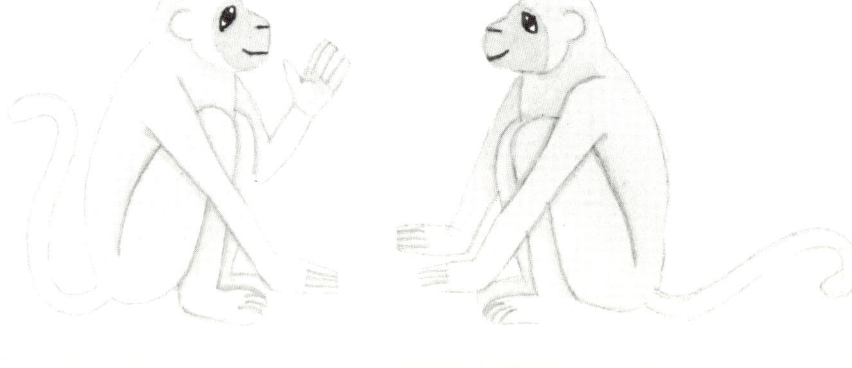

3

Hanuman, the Monkey Man

THERE WAS ONCE a prince called Rama who was married to a beautiful princess called Sita, whom he loved dearly. One day Sita disappeared. Rama was distraught, for he knew she would not have left him of her own free will. She must have been kidnapped – but who would do such a thing?

Rama knew of only one person who could help, and that was Hanuman. Hanuman was half man and half monkey, and general of the monkey army. With his magical powers he could shrink to the size of a mosquito, shoot up taller than a pine tree, shorten or lengthen his tail at will, and fly. Hanuman was strong and good, and used his powers to help those who were weak or in danger. He was the devoted friend and follower of Rama.

When Rama asked Hanuman to find Sita, Hanuman set his army of monkeys to look for her. The monkeys searched through the jungles and forests, in fields and on mountains, in tiny villages and great cities. Sita was nowhere to be found. Then Hanuman himself set out to look for her. With one great leap he soared up into the sky and flew all over India, scanning the land.

At last Hanuman came to the southernmost tip of the country, to the edge of the Indian Ocean. There on a cliff top he met the king of the eagles.

"I am looking for the princess Sita," said Hanuman. "Have you seen her?"

"Yes, I have seen her," said the king of the eagles. "Ravana, king of the demons, has taken her prisoner."

Hanuman had heard of the demon king. He had ten heads and twenty arms, and when he roared everyone trembled.

"Where has he taken her?" Hanuman asked.

The king of the eagles pointed across the sea with his wing. "Do you see that island on the horizon? That is Lanka. It is where the demons have built their city, and where Ravana's palace stands. It is surrounded by giants and demons with many heads. Sita is there, and she will never escape."

"I can rescue her," said Hanuman proudly, and thanking the king of the eagles, he leapt off the cliff and flew towards the island of Lanka.

In his haste to reach the palace of the demon king, he flew low, skimming across the sea. He did not notice the monster that reared up out of the water behind him, its huge jaws open wide. The monster saw Hanuman and lunged towards him. There was no time for him to fly out of reach. The monster opened its great mouth even wider, and swallowed him whole.

Hanuman felt himself sliding down a long tunnel; then he landed in a pool of water in the monster's vast stomach. All around him floated skeletons, broken masts and pieces of sail, the remains of ships the monster had swallowed.

Hanuman blew himself up like a balloon. He grew bigger and bigger, until he almost filled the monster's stomach. Then he began to jump about, poking and prodding at its sides. The monster felt uncomfortable and thrashed around in the sea, making huge waves. Hanuman was flung from side to side of the great dark cave of its stomach. Suddenly he caught a glimpse of light at the end of the tunnel; the monster had reared up out of the sea and opened its mighty mouth to get some air. Hanuman lost no time. He shrank to his normal size and flew up towards the opening of the tunnel, and before the monster knew what was happening, he had shot out of its mouth and was free.

Now Hanuman sped towards the shores of Lanka. He could see a great wall lining the beach, with hundreds of soldiers guarding it. He knew he could not get past them as he was, so he made himself shrink until he was even smaller than a mosquito, and flew right over the wall.

Within the walls lay the demon city. Giant warriors roamed its streets, carrying spears and clubs. Mighty elephants were lined up ready for war. Hanuman flew through the streets towards the palace, a magnificent building with golden domes and minarets.

It was night time. Guards watched the gates, but inside the palace everyone was asleep. Hanuman flew through room after room, all filled with gold furniture. In one room he saw the demon king's warrior son, Indrajit, sprawled on a great bed. In another room slept an ugly giant, Ravana's brother, who was said to sleep for six months of every year.

In the largest room of all Hanuman saw the demon king. He was lying on an enormous bed, his ten heads next to each other on a long pillow, each one snoring loudly, and his twenty arms stretched out, all at different angles.

Hanuman searched every room, but Sita was nowhere. At last he went out into the garden and there he found her. She was sitting under a tree in a circle of guards. Her beautiful face was sad, and he could see that she had been crying.

Hanuman alighted on the ground beside her, and softly whispered her name. He told her who he was and how he had come to find her. Sita was overjoyed, but she did not dare show her feelings in case the guards noticed.

Hanuman wanted to be caught, so that he could find out more about Ravana and the palace, and think of a way to rescue Sita. So he returned to his own size and started to walk back to the palace. The guards spotted him at once and ran towards him. Their shouts woke Ravana, and he sent his warrior son, Indrajit, out to fight with Hanuman. Indrajit brought his bow and arrow, and shot his arrows at Hanuman. The arrows were snakes, and Hanuman fell to the ground, caught up in their slithering coils.

Then Hanuman let himself be bound and taken to the demon king. Ravana was sitting on his golden throne, his ten heads and twenty arms all shaking with fury.

"You have annoyed me, monkey," said Ravana. "I am going to punish you."

The demon king knew that monkeys are proud of their tails, so he ordered his guards to set fire to Hanuman's. He told them to seize the tail, wrap cloth around it, pour oil on the cloth and set fire to it.

But as the soldiers did so, Hanuman made his tail grow longer and longer, till it trailed outside the door of the throne room. The soldiers ran to and fro, trying to keep hold of the tail and find more cloth to wrap it in and more oil to pour on it.

"Light the tail!" shouted Ravana, his ten heads glaring at the captive. An orange flame shot up from Hanuman's tail, but just then Hanuman began to shrink. The ropes that bound him

slipped to the ground. He stepped out of them and with a roar flew out of the palace, his tail alight.

When Sita saw Hanuman's tail burning she prayed to Agni, the god of fire, to save him. Hanuman realised the flames were doing him no harm, and he began to swish his tail about until the roof caught fire.

Soon the palace was ablaze. Hanuman leapt to the roof of a nearby house and set fire to it, then flew all over the city, setting fire to the houses of the demons. In a few moments the entire city was a mass of flame, with demons running in all directions to escape the fire.

Hanuman swooped down to the sea and dipped his tail in the water to put out the fire. He then soared away from Lanka and back to Rama, to tell him that Sita had been found.

The prince was overjoyed. He wanted to rescue Sita himself and with the help of his brother, Laxmana, he gathered an army together and made plans to march to Lanka and fight the demon king. The army was made up of monkeys, commanded by Hanuman, and bears, led by Jambavan their king.

They marched down to the south of India, to the edge of the ocean. Nala, a monkey who had the power to make stones float, built a bridge of stones for the animals to cross the ocean to Lanka, while Hanuman himself flew to the island with Rama upon his shoulders.

The demons were ready to fight. Ravana sent his best general to challenge Hanuman, but the monkey general simply lifted him with one hand, spun him round on his finger and threw him out of sight.

Next Ravana sent a huge giant into the fray. He was so ugly and ferocious that many of the animals in Rama's army ran away in terror at the sight of him, but Hanuman pulled a tree out of its roots and hit the giant with a resounding blow. The creature fell down unconscious, and as he hit the ground, hundreds of demon soldiers were crushed to death under his weight.

Then Rama's own brother, Laxmana, was wounded in the battle. A wise old monkey told Rama that the only thing that could save Laxmana's life was a special herb which grew on a mountain far away in the Himalayas.

Again Rama turned to Hanuman for help. Hanuman leapt into the air and flew to the mountain to pick the herb, but there were so many herbs growing there that he could not tell which was the right one. So Hanuman huffed and puffed and blew himself up until he was big enough to lift the whole mountain in his hand and carry it back to Rama. The old monkey doctor soon found the herb he wanted and cured not only Laxmana but also many other wounded soldiers in Rama's army.

Now the battle raged fiercer than ever, and Ravana himself joined the fight. Hanuman and the army of monkeys and bears fought bravely and killed many demons until at last Ravana and Rama faced each other.

Ravana attacked with a weapon in every one of his hands, but Rama moved like lightning, shooting a whole flight of arrows from his bow, and the demon king fell dead.

And so at last Rama and Sita were reunited and returned in triumph to their kingdom where there were feasts and celebrations for many days. The brave hero Hanuman was the guest of honour at the festivities and Sita, in gratitude, gave him her pearl necklace.

To this day people all over India remember Hanuman, and his statue can be found in temples and homes throughout the country.

4
The Story of Shakuntala

IN THE NORTH of India there once was a king called Dushyanta. One day he decided to go out hunting in the forest and there in a clearing he saw a young girl playing with the animals and birds. With her long hair and large black eyes, she was the most beautiful girl he had ever seen. He was immediately entranced and stopped to watch her.

"Who are you?" he asked. "And what are you doing here?"

"When I was a baby," the girl replied, giving him a radiant smile, "a wise man found me in the forest. The birds were feeding me, so he named me Shakuntala, which means 'birds' love'. He brought me home to this hut, and I have lived here as his daughter ever since."

Dushyanta had already fallen in love with this beautiful girl, and he decided there and then that he must marry her and take her back to his palace. Shakuntala protested that she could not marry and leave home without the blessing of her father, who was away on a long journey; but Dushyanta was so impatient to marry her that he insisted that the wedding should take place that very day, and he promised to stay with Shakuntala in the forest until her father came home.

Dushyanta and Shakuntala exchanged garlands, settled down in the hut, poor as it was, and were very happy together. They were so happy that Dushyanta forgot all about his kingdom and his responsibilities outside the forest: until one day his chief minister came to the hut and begged the king to return to his palace and rule his people as before.

Dushyanta reluctantly agreed, but Shakuntala would not go with him, for her father had still not returned. Sadly, the king said goodbye to his bride.

"Take this ring from my finger," he said to her as they parted. "It is a sign of my love for you, and proves that you are my wife. I will send for you, and if you come to my palace wearing this ring I shall know that you are truly my own Shakuntala."

Shakuntala took the ring and watched, weeping, as her husband rode away with his minister. When he was gone she

wandered into the forest amongst the wild creatures and sat down in a glade, holding the ring in her hands and dreaming of the day when she would be able to join her husband in his fine palace.

As she sat, lost in thought, a certain holy man called Durvashas came up to greet her. Now Durvashas was very wise and possessed great powers, but he was also irritable and bad-tempered. When Shakuntala ignored his greeting and continued to stare at the ring in her hand, Durvashas was angry. He wanted to punish the girl for her rudeness. He placed a curse on her, that whoever had given her the ring she cherished would forget her completely from that moment on.

Shakuntala did not even hear these words, but some friends of hers were sitting nearby, and pleaded with the wise man to withdraw his terrible curse. Shakuntala did not mean to ignore him, they said, but had thoughts only for her husband.

Durvashas could not remove his curse completely, but he did relent and agree to lessen it. The owner of the ring would forget Shakuntala, but if he ever saw the ring he would remember that he had given it away and recognise his bride.

Months passed. Shakuntala's father came home at last and was delighted to give her his blessing and agree to the marriage. Now she was free to leave home; but nobody came from the palace to fetch her. She was also expecting a baby, and longed to be with her husband. Still she waited.

"If nobody comes for me, then I shall have to go to the palace alone," said Shakuntala at last.

"You must ask some of your friends to go with you," said her father. "The journey is long and tiring and you should not travel on your own."

So Shakuntala said goodbye to her father, and set off with a group of her own friends towards the palace.

On the way they came to a river. It was so hot that the girls decided to go for a swim. While she was bathing in the water, Shakuntala's ring slipped off her finger, but she did not notice that it was missing.

Eventually she and her friends arrived at the palace. They were ushered into the grand hall where King Dushyanta sat on his throne.

"I have come to my home, your majesty," Shakuntala said. "I am your wife, Shakuntala, whom you married in the forest many months ago."

"But I have no wife," said Dushyanta, who had forgotten her completely, just as Durvashas had said he would.

"Here is the ring you gave me, as a sign of your love for me," Shakuntala cried, but when she looked down at her long, delicate hand the ring was gone from her finger! Her lips trembled. She knew that she could not prove that she was his wife, but it seemed as if he had completely forgotten her. Her friends watched her sadly, because they knew the awful truth. Durvashas' curse had come true, and without the ring Dushyanta would never remember his beautiful bride.

"Guards, remove this woman," said the king.

The guards pushed Shakuntala towards the door. Sorrowfully she walked out of the palace and started on the journey home, her friends at her side to comfort and support her.

A few months later Shakuntala gave birth to a handsome baby boy. She called him Bharat and he was born with a mark on his palm, shaped like a wheel, which was a sign of royal birth. Shakuntala taught him to read and write. He played with the wild beasts and birds in the forest and learnt how to hunt and fish, and how to fight. Shakuntala watched her son grow up strong, fine and intelligent. She told him who his father was and showed him how to behave like a real prince.

The years went by. One day one of Dushyanta's royal fishermen went fishing in the very same river in which Shakuntala had bathed on her way to the palace, and where she had lost her ring. The man caught a huge fish and knowing that the king would like it for his dinner, he took it straight back to the palace and showed it to him.

"Magnificent!" cried the king. "Give it to the royal cook and tell him to serve it tonight at my feast."

The fish was taken down to the kitchen and the royal cook laid it on a table to slice and prepare it. With his long knife, he slit it open. There in the fish's belly lay a gold ring, sparkling with precious jewels.

The cook placed the ring on a red cushion and hurried up to the grand hall to show it to the king. The moment Dushyanta saw it, he knew what it was.

"Where did you find it?" he demanded.

"In the belly of the fish I have cooked for your dinner, your majesty," replied the cook.

Suddenly, just as Durvashas had predicted, Dushyanta remembered Shakuntala and how he had given her the ring to prove that she was his wife, and he recalled the lady who had come to the palace all those years ago claiming to be his queen. She must indeed have been Shakuntala, but why hadn't he recognised her? Dushyanta was angry with himself for being so blind. He wished desperately to see his beloved wife. Immediately he sent his soldiers to the four corners of his kingdom to find her and bring her back, but they searched in vain and could not find her.

Dushyanta was heartbroken. He decided he must go and look for her himself, and try to find her in the forest where he had first caught sight of her in the clearing.

As Dushyanta rode into the forest, he glimpsed through the trees a young boy playing with some lion cubs. The boy was so handsome, he seemed like a prince. Dushyanta rode up to him and asked his name.

"My name is Bharat," the boy replied proudly.

"Who is your father?" asked the king.

"Why, King Dushyanta, of course," said the boy.

"And your mother?"

"My mother is Shakuntala."

Tears flowed down the king's cheeks. He was overjoyed.

"Will you take me to your mother?" he asked.

"Of course," said the boy. "Follow me."

He led Dushyanta through the trees to the hut where Shakuntala still lived. She hurried out to greet her son. Then she saw the king and stared at him in amazement.

"You are my wife!" cried Dushyanta. "I have searched for you everywhere! Forgive me, Shakuntala. You have been brave and noble, while I have been cruel and thoughtless. Please come back with me to the palace, where you and Bharat belong."

Shakuntala gladly said she would, and she and Bharat went with the king to his palace, where Shakuntala was treated with the respect that befits a queen.

And so the curse of Durvashas was at last overcome. Dushyanta, his wife and son all lived happily ever after. Shakuntala brought up her son so well that when he grew up he became one of the greatest rulers India has ever had. He was so fine a king, indeed, that the country itself was given Bharat's name and to this day Indians call their homeland Bharat.

হরে কৃষ্ণ

5
Krishna Tricks the Girls

THERE WAS ONCE a boy called Krishna, who lived with his father and mother in a village in the country.

Krishna looked different from the other children in the village. He was not just an ordinary boy, he was a god, and like many other Indian gods, his skin was blue. Everyone liked him because he was fun to be with and thought of exciting things to do. He was always full of mischief and loved playing tricks on people. If he was caught he would smile angelically and say he was sorry, and no one could be angry with him for long.

One day Krishna was out in the fields looking after the cows, when he heard a boy playing a flute. It made such a soft sweet sound that Krishna decided that he must have one for himself. He rushed home to his mother and begged her to buy him one.

"But who will teach you to play?" his mother asked.

"No one," said Krishna confidently. "I'll teach myself."

And so he did. His mother brought him a flute from the bazaar, and Krishna sat down under a tree, far away across the fields where no one could hear him, and tried to play. At first he could only make a funny squeaking noise, but every day he would sit under the tree and practise until at last he could play a tune. It was a merry little tune, soft and sweet, easy on the ear, the sort of tune you could listen to for ever. Krishna practised it and learned another, and another. Each tune was lovelier than the last.

One morning when Krishna was playing his flute, a little bird flew down to listen. It hopped right up to Krishna, its head cocked to one side so it could hear better. Another bird perched on a branch above his head to listen. Then some monkeys clustered round; and tigers, bears and elephants formed a circle around Krishna's feet, all charmed by his flute playing. Even the snakes slithered out from under the stones where they hid, and curled up within earshot of the music. Day after day Krishna would play his tunes, and the birds and animals would listen.

Now it was time for the Festival of Holi, when all over India the arrival of spring is celebrated. Holi is a time for music and laughter, singing and dancing. And it is the custom for people to throw coloured powder over the earth and shower each other with coloured water.

Just as the festival began, Krishna thought of a wonderful trick to play on the village girls. He called a secret meeting for the boys.

"Listen," said Krishna, "I have had a good idea. If you do exactly what I say, I promise you will see something very funny. First, I want each of you to bring me two buckets filled with coloured powders mixed with water – the brightest colours you can find. Then I will tell you what to do next."

The boys were puzzled, but they were used to doing what Krishna told them so they all ran back to their homes and brought Krishna buckets of water in all the colours of the rainbow.

"That's good," said Krishna, peering into the buckets. "Now, pick up the buckets and follow me."

He led the way towards the forest that lay on the outskirts of

the village, playing his flute as he went. The boys followed in a long line, carrying a bucket in each hand. Krishna stopped in a clearing.

"Now I want everyone to hide up in the trees. Climb up and find a strong branch to sit on. Take your buckets with you, making sure you don't spill them, and hide yourselves in the leaves and branches so you can't be seen."

Then Krishna told them his plan. The boys thought it was very funny and scrambled up into the trees to hide, laughing.

"Sssh! Don't let anyone hear you!" said Krishna. Sitting alone in the middle of the clearing, he took out his flute and began to play.

Softly, sweetly the notes came, soothing and pleasant to listen to. There was a hush in the forest, as boys, birds and beasts were still, listening to the flute. The music travelled through the forest, across the river, through the village and to the fields where the village girls were playing in the bright new dresses they had put on for the festival.

"Listen to that beautiful music! Where is it coming from?" asked one of the girls.

Radha, the liveliest and cleverest of them, stopped to listen.

"It must be coming from the village. Let's go and see what it is," she said.

The girls ran back to the village, but no one there was playing the flute. They ran further, crossed the river and went into the heart of the forest, led by the sound of the flute. At last they came to the clearing where Krishna sat playing.

When Krishna saw the girls coming he closed his eyes, pretending not to notice them. He played even more sweetly. The girls stood in the clearing, entranced by the sound of the flute.

"*Now!*" said Krishna suddenly, opening his eyes. The boys, perched up in the trees, tipped their buckets upside down. A shower of coloured water poured down over the girls, drenching their hair, their faces and their new dresses.

The girls ran around shrieking in surprise. "Oh! The monsoon rains have come early. Oh, what shall we do? Look at our nice new clothes! Oh, oh, oh!"

Then Krishna grinned a huge grin and the boys in the trees howled with laughter. "Happy Holi!" they cried.

When she saw Krishna laughing, Radha cried, "Oh, it's Krishna playing one of his tricks. We should have guessed it would be him!"

"I'm sorry, Radha," said Krishna, looking repentant. "I only meant to have a bit of fun with my flute, and as it's Holi and the first day of spring it seemed too good a chance to miss. Please for-

give me. Let's be friends." He smiled so charmingly and looked so sincere that the girls couldn't be angry.

"All right," said Radha. "It's only coloured water, and our dresses will soon dry in the sun. We'll be friends, just as long as you don't play any more tricks on us!"

Krishna picked up his flute with a smile, and played for them, and they danced and sang until it was time to return to their homes for the evening meal.

6
The Prince and the Fish

THERE WAS ONCE a king called Pandu, who had five sons. They were all fine and brave princes who had many adventures and fought great battles, but their worst enemies were their own cousins, the one hundred sons of Pandu's brother, who were jealous of their beauty, strength and wisdom.

It was common practice in those days for a king to renounce his kingdom and become a hermit, but when Pandu did so, his brother immediately seized the throne. The new king loved his wicked sons, and fearing that the people of the kingdom would prefer to be ruled by Pandu's sons instead of his own, he banished the five princes to the forest.

And there the sons of Pandu lived like holy men, dressed in skins and orange cloth. The eldest brother, Yudhishthira, was serious and wise; if any man was fit to be a king it was he. Bhima, the second, was as strong as a maddened elephant. The twins, Nakula and Sahadeva, were handsome and skilled with the sword. But the noblest of them all was the mighty Arjuna, fearless as a tiger and the greatest archer in all India.

Now the Rajah of Panchala had a daughter named Draupadi, whose hair was as black as night and whose eyes were shaped like two beautiful lotus petals. She was old enough to take a husband, but her father believed that there was only one man good enough for her . . . the noble Arjuna. And so the rajah decided to hold a special swayamvara.

He invited princes, kings, rajahs and maharajahs, who came from all over India hoping to be chosen as Draupadi's husband. They came in their hundreds, dressed in glittering jewels and silken robes, riding on majestic elephants or in golden chariots pulled by thoroughbred horses. Among those who came were Arjuna and his four brothers, but they were dressed only in the tattered robes of holy men.

The palace was full when Draupadi's father called out, "The man who wishes to marry my daughter must first perform a feat of skill."

The princes and rajahs stopped shuffling, the maharajahs and kings stopped chattering and they all listened eagerly.

"In the courtyard I have set up a target. It is a fish. Whoever knocks it down will marry my daughter. But first he must string this bow and shoot an arrow through the spinning metal wheel that hangs below the fish. This is not all. When he takes aim he must look not at the fish but at its reflection in the pool of water below it. The man who can accomplish this will be Draupadi's husband."

This was an almost impossible task, but everyone was eager to compete. One by one the kings, rajahs, princes and maharajahs stepped forward, and one by one they all failed to hit the fish. Some arrows flew off target and hit the walls, some hit the metal wheel but failed to pass through the holes, some princes could not manage to string the bow and others couldn't even lift the bow at all, it was so heavy.

At last every royal suitor had taken his turn and tried his luck, except one young man dressed in rags and skins. As the handsome Arjuna strode forward to take up the bow his ragged clothes could not conceal his noble bearing and strongly built body. The crowd fell silent. Arjuna paused and looked about him until his eyes met Draupadi's. They held each other's gaze and fell deeply in love.

Effortlessly the mighty warrior picked up the bow and strung it. Casting a practised eye over the arrows, he chose the straightest, fitted it to the bowstring and took aim in the water.

Arjuna fired so powerful a shot that the bow snapped with a loud crack! The arrow shot through the wheel and the fish fell to the ground like a stone.

"Ah, this is Arjuna!" cried the crowd. "Only the heroic Arjuna has such skill!" And they cheered and roared in admiration.

Blushing, Draupadi proudly placed a garland of flowers around Arjuna's neck as a bride should do. Her father too was overjoyed.

"Oh, noble Arjuna!" he cried. "I set up this test because I knew only you have the skill to accomplish such a feat. I could not have given my daughter to an unknown beggar dressed in skins without all these great lords wishing to kill me in their fury. Yet who would dare say the mighty Arjuna is not a suitable husband for my daughter?"

And so the brothers were dressed in fine clothes and precious stones, Draupadi was married in great splendour and the feasting and merriment lasted for many days.

Arjuna and his brothers had many more adventures and years later they fought a great battle in which they defeated their hundred wicked cousins and won the kingdom back. But that is another story.

7

King Poras Keeps his Promise

LONG, LONG AGO India was ruled by a great and noble king named Poras. In those days India was the richest and most splendid country in the world. Her people were prosperous and contented, many wore beautiful clothes and some lived in fine marble palaces.

Because of the gold and precious jewels that were rumoured to be in India, all the world's rulers wanted to own her. The greatest of these was Alexander, the emperor of the Greeks. Alexander was a fine warrior who had conquered many countries, and wanted to rule the entire world. He had set his heart on conquering India.

Poras too was a great warrior. He was also a good and kind ruler, and was determined never to allow his country to be invaded by another.

Now there was a woman Alexander loved, a beautiful Persian princess with blue eyes called Rukhsana. When she realised that he was set on conquering India, she was afraid, for King Poras' army was known to be strong and powerful. She decided to follow her beloved secretly to India, fearing for his life.

Wearing a veil over her face so that nobody could see that she was not an Indian woman, Rukhsana crossed the frontier and made her way to the city where Poras had his great palace. As she arrived there, she heard the sounds of merrymaking and laughter in the streets.

"Please, tell me what the celebrations are for?" she said to an old man who was passing.

"Don't you know, my dear, that today we are celebrating the Festival of Rakhee?" he repied. When she shook her head, he went on, "Rakhee means protection, and today is the day when sisters tie a special string on their brothers' wrists, and in return the brothers promise to protect them and grant them whatever they want. It is a most sacred and important day! Why don't you join in the festivities?"

But Rukhsana had already disappeared into the crowd, for a clever idea had struck her while the old man was speaking. She bought a rakhee string from the bazaar and then hurried to the palace. Entering the gates, she passed through many splendid rooms crowded with people in fine clothes. At last she came to the great hall, and there she saw the mighty ruler sitting on his throne, surrounded by his courtiers.

Rukhsana removed her veil and everyone stared as the beautiful and mysterious lady walked straight up to the king and tied the rakhee string on his wrist. There was silence in the hall.

At last Poras spoke. "Lady, you have the bluest eyes I have ever seen. You must come from some far off place. Who are you?" Rukhsana did not reply.

"Well," said Poras, "with this rakhee you have made me your brother. Whatever you wish for, it will be granted."

Then, holding her head high, Rukhsana spoke. "I ask you for the life of the emperor Alexander," she said. "He has come to this land to do battle with you, but I want you, as my brother, to promise that he will never be killed by your hand."

Now Indian rulers placed much importance on their word and their promise. It was a matter of great honour, and Poras paused for a moment. He looked at the proud and brave lady and replied, "Yes, oh fair one. You have tied this rakhee on me, and I have promised to grant your wish. I will do as you ask."

The courtiers looked at each other in amazement, but Poras held up his hand to show that he had given his word. Rukhsana bowed her head in gratitude to the noble ruler who sat before her, then turned and walked out of the palace.

Meanwhile, Alexander had crossed the Indian frontier and was marching inland at the head of his conquering army. However, his progress was not easy, for Poras' soldiers were well-trained and fearless, and everywhere there were scenes of fierce fighting and bloodshed.

At last, Poras himself drew up his mighty army of elephants, horses and men on the banks of a river, and prepared to face the invader in a great battle. Alexander the Great, wearing shining armour, rode at the head of his army on a snow-white horse. Poras rode on a huge elephant decked in gold and jewels. After many attempts Alexander and his men succeeded in crossing the river and attacking. The battle which followed raged for many hours with hundreds of men killed or wounded on both sides.

Eventually, Poras and Alexander drew up close to each other on their mounts, and prepared to fight man to man. All around the men stopped and stared. Soldiers moved away to make space for the two great rulers to fight. A hush fell over both armies as everyone watched and waited.

The two men turned about and rode hard towards each other, spurring on their steeds. They rode closer and closer, thundering across the ground which was wet and soft after the heavy monsoon rains.

Suddenly Alexander's horse slipped in some mud and its legs buckled, throwing the emperor forward onto the ground. The mighty conqueror was helpless. Poras raised his arm to throw his sharp spear at Alexander; he could hardly miss at this close range. But then he remembered his promise to Rukhsana. He had given his word of honour that Alexander would never die at his hand, the hand on which Rukhsana had tied a rakhee.

Poras' generals and soldiers watched, amazed, as Poras lowered his spear, turned his elephant and rode away.

And that is how Alexander the Great was saved from death by a promise – the word of honour which Poras gave to Rukhsana when she tied a rakhee bracelet on his wrist. In fact, the battle was

finally won by Alexander but he could see that Poras was a fine and honourable king and so he offered the Indian ruler a treaty. The two men became sound allies, and each admired the other greatly for his bravery, skills and noble character.

Rakhee is still celebrated in the month of August by Indians all over the world. Sisters tie an elegant bracelet on those whom they call their brothers, and in return their brothers promise them eternal protection and loyalty.

8
Thugsen's Revenge

LONG AGO, IN THE kingdom of Ujjain in India, there lived a king called Vikram who had five wives. His favourite was the youngest, Shashikala, and the other four queens were all very jealous of her.

King Vikram had no sons, so when it was announced that Queen Shashikala was expecting a child, the other queens were terrified that she might have a baby boy who would inherit the kingdom. They told the king that Shashikala had been spreading lies and evil gossip about him.

The king was shocked when he heard the story. He asked his youngest and favourite wife if what he had been told was true. Shashikala was so upset and surprised to see her husband's anger that she could not speak for fright, and the foolish king took her silence to mean that she was guilty. He ordered his chief courtier to take her into the jungle and abandon her there. Ignoring the pleas of Shashikala's friends, who loved her and knew she was innocent, the chief took her from the palace and left her in the deepest, most dangerous part of the jungle. A few loyal servants went with her, and not long afterwards Shashikala gave birth to a handsome baby boy, whom she called Thugsen.

Many years passed. Thugsen grew up tall, strong and fine-looking. He was quick to learn, and loved to tease people and play tricks. He was musical, too, and played the flute with such skill that even the birds and animals in the jungle would come to listen to his music.

One day Queen Shashikala was talking to one of her maids about her days in the palace and how she had been cruelly thrown out. Thugsen overheard their conversation, and persuaded his mother to tell him the whole story. And so he learnt that she was a queen, and he himself a prince.

Then Thugsen made a vow to his mother to take his revenge for the way she had been treated. "It is better to forgive and to forget," said Shashikala gently.

But Thugsen only replied, "Yes, mother, one day I shall forgive and forget, but first I am going to the palace, and I shall see that the king and his queens and that wicked courtier are taught a lesson."

Reluctantly Shashikala allowed her son to go. She gave him some food for the journey and a beautiful jewel, a ruby the size of a pigeon's egg. When they had said their goodbyes, Thugsen set off for the city where Vikram had his palace.

Before long, he was stopped by a group of robbers who demanded his money. "Of course, of course," he replied. "But what's the hurry? You are five and I am one, so why don't you first share some of my food?"

The robbers were hungry, so they agreed. Just as they were about to settle down to eat, Thugsen said, "Oh, I forgot to tell you that I never eat without first having a bath. Do you mind if I take a quick dip in the lake over there before I join you?"

The robbers agreed to his request, but told him to be quick. Thugsen stayed in the lake for so long that the thieves grew impatient. At last they saw him coming out of the lake, holding a beautiful jewel in his hand. It was the ruby his mother had given him, but Thugsen pretended that the lake was full of such jewels and that he had found this one at the bottom. The greedy robbers were so excited that they stripped off all their clothes and jumped into the lake.

Thugsen laughed out loud as he watched his captors rush into the water in their haste to find the jewels. He quickly found the place where the robbers had tied their horses and picked the best one for himself, setting the others free so that the robbers could not catch him.

That night Thugsen stood outside the king's palace, playing a soft, lilting tune on his flute. The melody was so soothing that soon all the palace guards had fallen asleep and Thugsen was able to enter the palace grounds unchallenged. He made his way up the main staircase and into the rooms where the queens lay sleeping. Silently he removed their jewellery and escaped out of the palace and into the narrow streets of the city. He had taken his revenge on the four queens and he was satisfied.

The next morning the palace was filled with the shrieks and

cries of the queens as each discovered that she had been robbed. The king offered a large reward to anyone who succeeded in capturing the thief, but nobody had any idea who the culprit might be. Thugsen was far too clever to give himself away and no one came forward to claim the reward.

The king sent for his chief courtier. "When will you catch this thief?" he shouted. "After he has robbed the entire city?"

"I shall find him myself, your majesty," stammered the courtier. "I shall forbid anyone to leave the city tonight, and I shall search every house until I catch him."

He sent the royal messenger to the market place to announce his plan. When Thugsen heard it he devised another trick.

Disguising himself as an old washerman, he set off for the river gate, carrying a load of washing in a large bag. Inside the washing was hidden all the jewellery he had stolen from the queens.

As he approached the gate, he was stopped by two soldiers. "Where do you think you're going?" one of them enquired.

"Please have pity on me, good sirs," Thugsen whined. "If I don't wash these clothes tonight, my family will starve tomorrow." The guards thought the old washerman looked harmless enough, and allowed him through.

As soon as Thugsen was clear of the city walls, he hurried down to the river. He knew that it would not be long before the chief courtier heard that a washerman had been allowed to leave the city. He would guess the truth and come after Thugsen. This was just what Thugsen wanted to happen, for he had thought up an ingenious plan.

Soon he heard the sound of a horse's hooves, as the courtier galloped towards the river. Thugsen took from his bag a large, hollow melon and threw it into the river with a splash. The court-

ier saw a round shape bobbing in the water, just like a man's head.

"Stop thief!" he cried. "You cannot escape this time!" He tied his horse to a tree, threw off his clothes and dived into the river in pursuit. When he caught hold of the melon, and saw what it was, he realised he had been tricked. Blind with anger, he returned to the bank, only to find that his horse and his clothes were missing.

Crafty Thugsen had put on the courtier's clothes while he was in the water, and ridden back to the city pretending to be the courtier himself. He told the guards at the palace gates that an old man without any clothes was approaching and was the thief the king was searching for.

When the chief courtier arrived at the gates on foot, shivering with cold, the guards seized him and dragged him off to the king; but the king took one look at the prisoner and saw that they had all been tricked.

"This is not the thief. This man is none other than my chief courtier!" he cried. "Let him go!"

The courtier told his master the whole story. The king was angrier than ever. He had to go off on a hunting expedition for a few days, but he vowed that, when he returned, he would go after the culprit himself and capture him. The whole city buzzed with the news, but Thugsen smiled to himself, for now he had thought up a way to trick the king himself.

He disguised himself as a royal messenger, and went to the courtier to tell him that the king had commanded him to join the hunting expedition.

As the courtier rode into the jungle, accompanied by Thugsen in his disguise, Thugsen said, "I think it would be best if I ride on ahead and tell the king that you are on your way. You can easily follow this path to the camp."

The courtier agreed, for he was finding it hard keeping up with the royal messenger. Thugsen rode ahead to the king's camp and told him that the courtier had set off from the city, and that he had caught the thief.

The king was delighted. "This is marvellous news," he said, "but where is the courtier?"

"He is resting after an exhausting chase to catch the thief. I came on ahead," Thugsen replied.

Meanwhile, the courtier had become hopelessly lost, for the path Thugsen had shown him led not to the king's camp but to the deepest and thickest part of the jungle. Thugsen led the king to the same spot, promising him that he would meet his courtier just a few yards further on.

Soon the king too was in difficulty, just as Thugsen had planned. He turned to the king and said, "I'm afraid we'll have to

dismount and walk, your majesty. The jungle here seems too thick to continue on horseback."

They started walking, but when it grew dark Thugsen quietly slipped away to where his horse was tied, leaving the king alone in the forest. As he rode back to the city, he roared with laughter, saying, "Oh, father, how grateful I am to you for allowing me to grow up in the jungle!"

Morning was breaking when the tired and hungry king and his courtier finally met. They realised at once that they had both been tricked. It was many hours before the two men found their way out of the jungle and wearily returned to the palace.

The king now made an announcement to his people, saying that he was very impressed by the cunning of the young man who had managed to fool even his majesty and therefore he had decided to grant him a royal pardon. If he would show himself at the palace, the king would honour the man with a pardon and a handsome reward.

The following day the great hall was packed with people who wanted to see who this cunning man was. When everyone was assembled, the king stood up and addressed his subjects. "We are all most anxious to meet the clever thief who has deceived the four queens, the chief courtier and myself. Will he now present himself?"

"I am the one," said Thugsen, stepping forward from the crowd.

"Who are you?" said the king.

"I am the prince of Ujjain – your own son!" Thugsen replied.

"Young man," said the king, "I admire your daring spirit, but this is going too far!"

But Thugsen continued. "I speak the truth. My mother is none other than Queen Shashikala whom you unjustly banished seventeen years ago. My tricks on you have been to attract your attention and demand justice. My mother was innocent – she was the victim of the four queens' jealousy."

When the king heard these words, he knew that this tall young man was speaking the truth. He stepped down from his throne and embraced Thugsen. "Forgive me, my son," he said. "I realise now how your mother was wronged."

King Vikram ordered a special chariot to bring Thugsen's mother from the jungle, and at last father, mother and son were reunited. The old king decided to retire, and gave the throne to Thugsen.

Thugsen ruled wisely and well for many years, and his mother and father spent the rest of their days living happily and quietly together. As for the four queens and the chief courtier, they were banished from the kingdom of Ujjain for ever.